Strategic Spelling

Strategic Spelling
Every Writer's Tool

Liz Simon

HEINEMANN
Portsmouth, NH

Heinemann

A division of Reed Elsevier Inc.

361 Hanover Street

Portsmouth, NH 03801–3912

www.heinemann.com

Offices and agents throughout the world

The author and publisher wish to thank those who have generously given permission to reprint borrowed material:

"Miss Mary Mac, Mac, Mac" and "Chicken and Chips" are reprinted with permission from *Really Rapt* by Susan Hill. Published by Era Publications, Australia.

Clipart from Microsoft's Design Gallery and *Art Explosion, Volumes 1 and 2* by Nova Development Corporation.

Library of Congress Cataloging-in-Publication Data

Simon, Elizabeth Ann.

 Strategic spelling : every writer's tool / Liz Simon.

  p. cm.

 Includes bibliographical references.

 ISBN 0-325-00589-3 (pbk.)

1. English language—Orthography and spelling—Study and teaching. 2. Individualized instruction. I. Title.

LB1574.S52 2004

372.63'2—dc22   2003018542

Editor: Lois Bridges

Production: Lynne Reed

Cover design: Catherine Hawkes, Cat & Mouse

Typesetter: Valerie Levy/Drawing Board Studios

Manufacturing: Steve Bernier

Printed in the United States of America on acid-free paper

08 07 06 05 04 EB 1 2 3 4 5

To Tony, Alicia, Justine, and Christian

CONTENTS

ACKNOWLEDGMENTS

I defer to Marie Clay, who has greatly influenced my views about how children learn to read and write.

I want to thank Maria Chemis (Reading Recovery tutor). I have used many of her literacy ideas for children who are beginning school not only in this book, but in the classroom. Children feel very secure in this supportive environment, in which everything is modeled before the children "have a go."

I would like to acknowledge Alicia Goodall for her handwriting ideas. Using her program, children coordinate the senses of sight and hearing with hand movement. I have seen children who early in their schooling found letter learning difficult. When this handwriting procedure was implemented, they became confident writers of letters, words, and stories by the end of their first year of school.

Thank you also to Sandi Hawke, Cathy Gerner, Bob Bowden, Tara Smallze, Alicia Goodall, and Tony Simon for their assistance in editing and their suggestions for additions, computer information, and changes to the first draft. I especially want to thank Tony Simon for all the computer work he did getting this manuscript to the editor.

Strategic Spelling

Introduction

Sound and symbol spellers, word spellers, and language spellers are discussed in this book in separate chapters. In reality, most children's spelling development will overlap these categories. While children are learning to recognize and write their letters, they may at the same time be writing and spelling words or parts of words in phrases or sentences. While children are spelling high frequency words and their knowledge of spelling patterns is developing, they may also be developing knowledge about morphemes and syntactic constructions, for example.

Chapter 2: Sound and Symbol Spellers

- The beginning premise is that children come to school knowing the sound of their names.
- The first sound of their names, and later days of the week, are isolated and linked to the appropriate symbol (letter).
- Oral language, modeling, and later, writing—especially handwriting—get children on the road to recognizing and writing letters and using strategies such as listening and looking at the first sound of a word.
- Reinforcement activities and continual assessment are also part of this chapter.

Chapter 3: Word Spellers

■ The focus is on an individual spelling program; this allows children to learn at their own pace and developmental level. In higher grades, individual programs assist children's self-esteem because they generally involve a personal interaction between the child and the teacher.

■ A variety of strategies are emphasized, and children choose the most appropriate strategies for a particular word.

■ Children refer to a self-help strategy map.

■ Assessment analyzes exactly what strengths the child has and where problems lie.

Chapter 4: Language Spellers

■ Since children are now becoming conventional, accurate spellers, the focus is on word forms—knowledge about words associated with grammatical structures.

■ Children are challenged to think in various ways about word and language structures and to increase their vocabulary knowledge.

■ Children proofread; they learn to identify and habitually correct spelling and grammatical errors. Shared and individual writing are the natural contexts in which proofreading and self-correction processes are demonstrated and used by children.

Spelling Nuances

Spelling has always been a controversial area of learning. Some educators argue that it doesn't matter if a person spells correctly—computers correct spelling errors anyhow! People in the community argue that spelling is extremely important and see children's not being able to spell words correctly as an example of a lax education system.

Educators over time have held various beliefs. Some theorize that phonics is the strategy to use. Some advocate that spelling is simply a case of memorization or that children learn to spell incidentally when reading and writing.

Learning to spell is difficult because English words usually have more sounds than letters. As well as the forty-four individual letter sounds, there are varying numbers of letter combinations. A language like Italian is easier for young spellers—there is a consistent one-on-one match between individual letter sounds and whole-word sounds and more frequently a grapheme, phoneme match. The same factors that control spelling difficulty may also influence reading difficulty. Phonic methods are suited to orthographies such as Italian, but a language like English, which is also determined by logographics, will require more than a purely phonetic approach.

Because many words and parts of words are phonetically determined, phonological awareness is emphasized in English spelling, but listening only for sounds in words can create its own problems for writers and readers. For example, children often leave out vowel sounds because the consonants "fall in" on vowels and mask them (*pirate*). Vowels have short and long sounds, and there are vowel/vowel (*oo*) and vowel/consonant (*ow*) digraphs. And look at all the different sounds and pronunciations associated with the letter pattern *ough*. Homophones present problems, as well; the words have the same sound, but they have different spellings and meanings. Not to mention multiple-meaning words (homographs), which are spelled *and* sound the same—for example, *cataract* or *forge*. Noam Chomsky (1968) argues that English spelling is not an adequate system for representing sounds, [it is an] efficient system for representing meanings [and] morphemic relationships.

Somehow lists of words involving rote learning/memorization seem to go hand in hand with numerical scores. Children who can remember how to spell a list of twenty words correctly are often considered "good" spellers. Some children's visual perceptions are mature and they recall symbol sequences with ease. Some children may correctly spell words in lists but do not correctly reproduce them in their writing. Some children have difficulty recollecting spelling words in lists *and* in their writing. Examine lists of spelling words often given as homework. Are the words chosen at random? Are the words the same for all the children in the classroom? If lists

- do not reflect learning that has happened in the classroom and/or

■ are not differentiated (individualized) for varying levels of development,

then children who have poor visual perception—who are unable to recall letter sequences and word structures—will fail, because all they can resort to is guessing the spelling of the word.

Some children do learn to spell incidentally when reading and writing. There can, however, be a danger that these children may be writers who use only the words they feel safe with. Irene Fountas and Gay Su Pinnell ask about reading, "Is the text consistently so easy that children have no opportunity to build their problem-solving strategies?" The same could be asked of writing tasks given to children; do they extend a child's knowledge about words and vocabulary?

Listening only for phonemes, memorizing a list of words, or relying on incidental learning does not give children opportunities to learn about patterns or orthographic rules that govern the way we spell. Emphasizing one learning theory does not take into account the idiosyncrasies of English words. Spellers need to know that if one problem-solving operation is inadequate, then there are alternative ways for them to tackle the problem.

Spelling accuracy is a gradual process. There cannot be one method of learning to spell words, nor can spelling be considered an isolated operation; reading, writing, and spelling activities are the contexts within which children gradually learn to spell. Reading and writing are interrelated. When a child reads and writes, there are expectations (for example, where to start and what follows); children attend to visual detail; and they visually perceive, which means the brain searches for information, interprets it, processes its complexity (linking it to prior experience), integrates other information sources, and comes to a decision. Especially while writing, children develop directional behavior, one-on-one matching, and word-discovery techniques; discover the relationships among letters, words, and speech; and form understandings of how words work.

Another truth about spelling is that a child needs to develop more than one system—a multisensory approach—for identifying and distinguishing letters and words. Learning to spell involves understanding and using strategies—analyzing words, creating hypotheses, forming analogies, seeing relationships, perceiving and being flexible enough to deal with differences and unusual spellings. Competent spellers are *strategic spellers;* essentially, they listen to and dissect words and make phonetic, visual, syntactic, semantic, and etymological connections. All spellers need to be made aware of strategies and they need lots of practice writing and spelling in meaningful contexts in order to use these strategies.

The Purpose of Spelling

Learning to spell is necessary because:

- Words are the tool of the writer and they must be accurate.
- Accurate spelling enables writers to fluently express messages that are easily read and understood by others—writers and readers of English have common expectations about spelling conventions.
- Accurate spelling is part of the overall process of learning language. Expanding knowledge about words impacts the whole scheme of printed language (see Figure 1.1).

Spelling Development Indicators

Mimicry (visual writing) Young children see people writing and attempt to copy symbols. They make *visual* interpretations of writing.

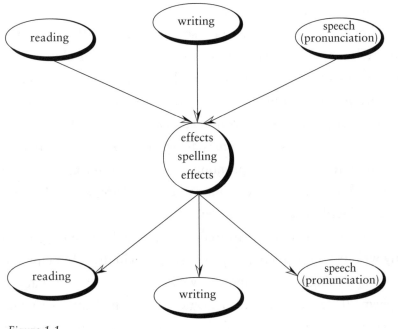

Figure 1.1

Pretending they are writing, children may scribble randomly or produce strings of scribbling. They may write two or three symbols:

aolaolaol aolaolaolaol (I love you, Mom)

These symbols can alternate:

aol loa aol loa (I have a car)

Early writers may write *random letters,* overusing certain letters. Letters may be assigned without much regard to matching letter–sound sequence. Often the letters are from the child's name:

M l o o r rr M (I went to town)
[The child's name is Mark.]

Children may produce a "story" letter by letter, or they may copy words without being aware of the associated sounds. Early writers may or may not know the difference between a drawing and writing.

Phonetic spelling   The first conscious analysis and attentive stage of spelling is *phonetic* spelling. Children may begin by relating sounds to symbols. Strategies teachers impart to children are looking, listening, and writing the first letter of a word.

Phonetic spelling is based on sound. Although they may not always reflect conventional English spelling, the words children write often represent successive main sounds—for example, children spell the word *jump* as *jm* or *jup* or *jum*. Phonetic spellers often omit nasal consonants (*n, m*)—for example, *went* may be spelled *wet*. They may add extra letters—*going* may be spelled *gowing*. Past tenses may be represented as they are pronounced: *lookt* for *looked, playd* for *played*. There may be a close match between letters and all essential sounds, placed in sequential order.

Developing phonemic awareness is essential for emergent and early writers (and readers). Teachers support children by helping them listen for (1) single unit sounds, as well as phoneme (sound) and grapheme (letter) correspondence, and (2) speech clusters—rhymes (*at,* hat, chat; *in,* bin, chin; *ake,* cake, rake), syllables, blends (*clap, strip*), and suffixes (*-ing, -ful*). Reading stories; doing finger plays; and reciting rhymes, jingles, and poems are activities that allow children to hear the sounds and rhythms of language.

Invented spelling Some theorists point out that when children are spelling phonetically and throughout their transition from phonetic to visual spelling, they write words that approximate the correctly written form and that these approximations, or *inventions,* should be accepted and encouraged as a natural part of learning to spell. It is a time when children take risks, experiment, and explore; they attempt to find patterns and an order in the English spelling system. It is "in the process of inventing that children learn what English orthography will and will not allow" (Bean and Bouffler 1997).

As with spoken language, spelling develops as children experiment, imitate, discuss, and are given feedback that helps them refine their knowledge about words. Praise and feedback provide important encouragement for children to "have a go" at spelling and develop an understanding of the complex English spelling system. Children may spell some words or parts of words with confidence and hypothesize others. How you react to their spelling attempts will influence their next try. Oral praise and checking off (✔) parts of words a child has spelled correctly, coupled with the careful choice of strategies to use in the future, shows a child how to get his or her invented words closer to the correct form.

Conventional spelling—visual, semantic, and accurate A conventional speller can automatically spell a large body of words correctly. A conventional speller has the ability to systematically visualize and internalize letter sequences and structures of words, as well as mentally store and retrieve them. Conventional spellers are able to recognize when a word doesn't look right and think of alternative spellings. They know what is right in context—for example, *site* or *sight.* They know about vowels in every syllable, double consonants, and silent letters; they understand and use grammatical conventions. Conventional spellers have moved from reliance on phonological information to visual and morphological (form and structure) information—for example, compound words, silent consonants, contractions, prefixes, suffixes, and derivatives. Conventional spellers attempt new words by making use of prior knowledge; they can look at a word and know something is wrong and they know how to help themselves. Indications like these mean a child is on the road to becoming a confident, conventional speller.

Guiding Strategic Spelling

If words are the writer's tool, then learning to spell them must be embedded in all areas of English language learning—reading, writing, and speaking. Spelling should not be isolated from the literacy whole.

Accurate spelling requires that children know how to solve problems by using certain strategies when they are writing. Strategic spellers become familiar with the patterns and inconsistencies of English words and act on that knowledge. Children can become strategic spellers if literacy programs and classroom practices focus on knowledge and strategies that will increase success for all children. Through many exposures to print and many experiences with writing, children see how the words they are learning to spell are used.

Learning to spell takes place within meaningful and sensible situations when:

- *Written models* are used to generate discussion about words and consequent strategies to use. These models are:

    Shared reading.

    Shared writing, to include *interactive* and *guided writing.*

- Opportunities for practice are provided within which *effective feedback* is given:

    Independent writing.

    Reinforcement activities.

    Individual spelling.

    Analytical assessment.

Shared reading   Shared reading using enlarged text—for example, big books, poems, charts, and labels—is a supportive reading experience that lets a large group of children make easy visual contact with the text. During shared reading the teacher leads the reading and subsequent learning and discussion. Shared reading allows all children to experience a range of texts and literacy language and provides teachers with opportunities to model, demonstrate, converse, question, and confirm knowledge in a secure environment.

Words in the text are singled out for study, and spelling strategies are demonstrated. Teaching spelling through shared reading not only provides models of correct spelling, it shows children the techniques that writers use to make their meaning clear and exposes them to the vocabulary employed to explain, create, and tell. Shared reading sparks an interest in words and develops language competence. Spelling makes more sense and is more stimulating for children when examples are shown in a piece of text rather than shown in isolation. Specific, intentional study of words and their spellings takes place at a regular time each day in the context of shared, guided, and independent reading of continuous print.

Writing Early writing focuses on the smallest elements—letters and the sequencing of letters. Children build their lexical and syntactic knowledge through extensive experience with literacy, especially when generating continuous language to put into print.

During shared writing (modeled, joint construction of text), as a teacher constructs a piece of writing in front of the class words and strategies are explored. Children look for critical features of words—predictable sequences of letters, common patterns, and the irregular features that differentiate each word from other words. The teacher's emphasis during shared writing is to extend a child's vocabulary and knowledge about sentence structures, helping the child think about how she can problem-solve the spelling of new or difficult words. For example:

- Say the word slowly as it is being written.
- Listen and look at the letter sequence. As the word is being said, write the corresponding symbol in sound boxes to show graphophonic relationships.

- Look carefully to see visual patterns:

cake rough

- Relate the known word to another similar word and link words by pointing out the constant parts:

me he is in

- Encourage children to find new words and their meanings.
- Use visual memory to determine whether a word looks correct.
- Write and spell the word syllable by syllable.

■ Demonstrate how children are responsible writers—show them where they can go to seek help when unsure about spelling (word lists and dictionaries, for example).

After a shared writing session, while the majority of the class is writing independently, a teacher can guide a group of emergent writers in interactive writing. This form of supportive, shared small-group writing is especially effective for introducing the writing process to new or unsure writers. It not only quickens the "learning to write" process, but allows differential (individual) learning to take place. With teacher support, a small group of children (approximately six) suggest ideas and "share the same pen" to construct text they would not be able to do alone.

The children first think of an idea, and each child takes a turn writing words or parts of words on a large sheet of paper or on a white- or blackboard. Children learn to begin sentences with capitals and finish with periods, to use spaces, to recognize directional behavior, and to develop strategies for problem-solving the spelling of words. The teacher could have the children write beginning phrases such as *I am, I can, I like,* and *I went* and later insert *he can, Mom likes,* or *dad went* or extend the sentences by adding *and.* (Use repetitively written texts as models.)

After shared writing, when the class is absorbed in the writing task, the teacher can also convene a small group for guided writing. (Guided writing is not only a technique for supporting older reluctant writers, but also one that will extend the more able writer's thinking, inventiveness, and expertise.) As the children write using their own pens and paper, the teacher discusses and demonstrates on a small whiteboard the thinking processes the children need to structure their writing. Or she shows the group spelling strategies (see the shared writing discussion) and other aspects of writing—for example, placing adjectives before nouns to add interest to texts, adding conjunctions to create compound sentences, and writing capitals at the beginning of new sentences and periods at the end of sentences. After the initial one or two sentences, the group then independently continues the writing task.

Children need to write every day and experiment with forms of writing in which their spelling understanding and fluency is developed and extended; they will continually recall prior knowledge as they tackle new words. Children must be encouraged to write even when they can't spell accurately, since attempting to spell is part of the learning process.

Educational writers talk about developing an attitude toward spelling as children read and write—a "spelling conscience." The expectation is that children pay serious attention to words, that they form the habit of *looking carefully at words, proofreading,* and *correcting.* Proofreading is a self-corrective behavior; it is an essential part of a child's writing regimen. From the very earliest writing, children should get into the habit of rereading their writing; later they can circle words they think are incorrectly spelled and later again, they can consult dictionaries to correct unsure spelling.

Competent writers generally tend to articulate their words clearly, and their handwriting is fluent and legible. Any aspect of writing the child agonizes over dulls the desire to produce written language and develop a spelling conscience. Learning to speak clearly and handwrite legibly are also important aspects that affect children's spelling attempts.

Individual spelling   "Knowing some two hundred words in a basic sight vocabulary gives immediate access to 30–40 percent of running English" (Holdaway 1979). At a certain stage in a child's spelling development he or she needs to learn high frequency words quickly. Children will learn these words at varying speeds, and an individual spelling program allows children to learn at their own pace. Known and unknown words are assessed. As unknown words are learned, strategies are discussed—for example, linking new words to known words; matching letter sounds with symbols; looking closely at initial letters, endings, and medial letters, as well as double letters and unusual parts; and knowing the meanings of words. When children read and write, they make connections with the words and strategies they have learned.

Reinforcement activities   The teacher generates specific spelling tasks from shared reading, shared writing, and individual spelling. Children are able to choose word studies that they find most helpful and compelling, that not only reinforce and extend their spelling knowledge and achievement but provide opportunities to learn more than they already know. For example, children may have studied the *ay* digraph from a big book and the teacher is then able to extend the learning in a game that introduces the digraph *ai* (the same sound, but a different look).

Assessment   Marie Clay, in her book *An Observation Survey,* states that when assessing, we should "use tasks that are close to the learning tasks of the classroom [rather than standardized tests] to observe what children have been able to learn, to discover what . . . they should . . . be taught [next]." Analyzing spelling miscues provides information about the strategies a child is using, his or her lexical knowledge, and whether the child is at an appropriate spelling level. Analysis shows what part of the word the child can or cannot master. For example, by examining invented words in children's writing, teachers gain insights into how the writer is tackling spelling and use this knowledge to:

■ Devise plans that move children through and out of each transitional level of spelling into the next; make clear and knowledgeable choices concerning teaching and learning experiences, as well as the grouping of students and resources to use.

■ Create an instructional plan that includes something worth learning and knowing about spelling. Plans include whole-class focuses and learning at the point of need for groups and individual children.

■ Create an instructional plan in which words are grouped by visual aspects, sounds, and structural and meaning similarities. For example:

Symbol and sound relationships.

Vowels.

Double letters.

Silent letters.

Frequently used words in text.

Multisyllabic words.

Plurals.

Common verbs—past, present, regular, and irregular.

Prefixes and suffixes.

Homonyms.

Semantic base words and derived forms.

Visual patterns.

Classroom Strategies for Sound and Symbol Spellers

As children are reading, writing, and participating in spelling activities at this level, they are learning about directionality, letters, matching sounds to letters, one-on-one matching, and the sequence of letters in words.

Most new learners come to school with effective "free-range" oral communication and visual perceptual systems; they have gradually learned, in small steps, how to perceive and make sense of their world and how to communicate their wants and ideas. Although most preschool children have developed good visual perception and oral language, they scan print fairly haphazardly and their oral language does not necessarily relate to the written word. When children begin school, new demands are made of them. They face new problems requiring more attention to detail; they need to harness their *modus operandi* into more formalized behavior. They must learn precise directional behavior for print, words, and letters; understand the relationships of sounds and symbols; match the oral word to the written word; and much more.

As soon as children begin school, they should be encouraged to write every day. Children should not be pressured into formal writing, but after each class shared session or small-group interactive session, they can experiment by drawing pictures, "toying" with writing, and being encouraged to write initial sounds of words or invent words. This can be done on paper using pencils, crayons, or paint; on white- or blackboards; and by writing letters and words in sand.

Children need a supportive environment in which they feel that taking risks and launching out into new learning is safe. A program that initially involves lots of modeling—seeing, showing, and sharing; practicing saying words and listening to the sounds—supports a new entrant to school when moving into the next phase of learning.

Do not assume that all children understand the language you use to direct them to listen and look at specific parts—for example, *first, last, middle, up, down, bottom, top, start, begin, space, round,* or *below.* Assess their concept knowledge by using the Boehm Test of Basic Concepts and reinforce these and other concepts (letters, words) during shared reading, writing, and reinforcement activities. You may have to teach some concepts explicitly using games and exercises in which the concept is an action the children perform.

**GUIDING STRATEGIC SPELLING FOR SOUND
AND SYMBOL SPELLERS:**

Written models:

Shared reading.

Shared writing, to include interactive writing.

Opportunities for practice:

Independent writing, handwriting.

Reinforcement activities.

Shared Reading

Big Books

Big books are specially designed for shared reading. Children can easily see the generous-size print and they love rereading these books because of the rhyme, repetition, and eye-engaging illustrations. The first day the book is introduced, emphasize constructing meaning, who the characters are, the episodes, and how the events may relate to the children's own experiences. Discussion, comments, predictions, and suggested outcomes should all be part of the initial reading. Once the text is familiar to the children, start teaching specific skills. Remember, by adapting parts of established texts during shared writing, you can make your own big books.

Plan ways to highlight the spelling focus. For example, you may be using the big book *In the Tall, Tall Grass,* by Denise Fleming. Once the story is familiar to the children, you hone in on the teaching focus, which in this case is the initial letter of a word—the letter *t* (the examples in the book are *tall*, *tug*, *tongues*). You could begin by using a window device that shows only the particular letter and on another occasion ask meaning-based questions, such as "What is a word on this page that begins with *t* and tells you it is high in height?"

Rhymes, Poems, and Chants

Words rhyme when they share common sounds: *at* in cat, hat, mat; *eg* in leg, peg, beg; *ing* in sing, ring, wing. Educators believe there is a strong link between rhyme knowledge and subsequent phonological awareness and the construction of analogies, especially alliteration and the latter parts of words—the *rimes*.

➡ Rhymes always appeal to children. Rhymes like "Twinkle, Twinkle Little Star," "Little Jack Horner," and "Mary Had a Little Lamb" can be repeated as the children use pointers or their eyes to follow the movement of words left to right and the return sweep at the end of a line.

The spelling program can begin with a significant piece of print that children are likely to know—their names. The sound and look of the letters at the beginning of children's names are meaningful starting points for sound and symbol spellers.

➡ Write a name poem in big print, and ask the children to follow the words as they read.

When I was little,   I have a name
as little as can be   And you have one too
I was given a name   But mine means me
and my name   And yours means you.
means me

➡ Have a child look in a mirror as you read the poem "I Looked in the Mirror."

I looked in the mirror   A mouth and a nose
and what did I see?   Could that be
A smiling face . . .   [   ]
Could that be me?   Do you suppose?
Two eyes, two ears

➤ Emphasize the beginning letters of day names by reading the poem "What Did I See" (written in big-print) during shared reading.

Monday, Monday. What did I see?

I saw a black dog looking at me.

Tuesday, Tuesday. What did I see?

I saw an orange cat looking at me.

Wednesday, Wednesday. What did I see?

I saw a red bird looking at me.

Thursday, Thursday. What did I see?

I saw a brown monkey looking at me.

Friday, Friday. What did I see?

I saw a white horse looking at me.

Saturday, Saturday. What did I see?

I saw a green parrot looking at me.

Sunday, Sunday. What did I see?

I saw nothing looking at me!

➤ Encourage clear pronunciation when reciting speech rhymes and chants. Hearing all the sounds as the words are being said is important when children are spelling.

A sailor went to sea sea sea
To see what he could see see see
And all that he could see see see
Was the deep blue sea sea sea.

(Unknown author)

Four funny men
They went to bed
With four, furry, funny hats
Upon each head.

(Unknown author)

Miss Mary Mac, Mac, Mac,
All dressed in black, black, black
With silver buttons, buttons,
   buttons,
All down her back.

Chicken and chips
Chicken and chips
Everybody here likes
   chicken
and chips.

(from Really Rapt, *chants compiled by Susan Hill)*

Charts and Alphabet Books

➥ Use an alphabet chart (see black line master, p. 81) to demonstrate looking at the initial letter and listening for the initial sound. Configure the letters to match the lines of the song "ABC."

ABCD
EFG
HIJK
LMNOP
QRSTUV
WXYZ
Now I know my ABCs, won't you come and sing with me.

Black Line Master: Letter Chart—Line configuration of the "ABC song"

As the alphabet is being sung each day, the children begin to connect sounds and symbols and directional behavior is modeled. Use a removable set of letters when you need to emphasize a letter—for example, the first letter of a child's name.

Follow up by reading little letter books (the *Dominie* letter books, for example).

➡ Write each child's name on a card for him or her to wear. For a week, have the children select their name tags from an alphabetically ordered name chart (use Velcro or a similar adhesive to attach names to the chart). Later, they can find other children's names on the chart.

➡ Children's names can be used on all sorts of charts. For example:

Birthdays   **Who is here today?**   **Helpers**

➡ Make a day chart. Read this chart each day. Have children interact with the chart by pointing at each word.

Today is _____ .

I am here today.

Continue using these literacy activities to reinforce reading names and relating sounds to letters. Also, point out examples, ask questions, and introduce reinforcement activities (see p. 28) to support growing knowledge about directionality, one-on-one matching, the concept of letters, and the first letters of words.

Shared Writing, Independent Writing, and Handwriting

Shared Writing

Every day, model writing phrases and sentences in front of the children. Write in large print and encourage children to verbally give what spelling they can—especially the initial letter. You can begin shared writing (whole class and small interactive writing groups) by constructing repetitive phrases. Talk about where to start, directionality, and the use of capital letters and periods. Introduce the concepts of letters and words by showing how letters make words.

➡ As a shared writing lesson make a "name" big book. The children first draw pictures of themselves on large sheets of paper. On three or four pictures on consecutive days, as the children look on, write the caption "I am _____ " under each face. Later, children can write the phrase and their names under your writing.

➡ Take photographs of the children playing in the schoolyard and make an "I can _____ " book showing the actions they are performing. Write "I can _____ " alongside each photograph. Write captions on cards and put them in an envelope at the back of the book; have the children match the captions with the pictures and then read the phrases.

➡ Take photographs on special days at school and make a class book.

"**Today at school** _____ "

I made	⬜	I made	⬜
_____ _____		_____ _____	

➡ Make different structured books—for example, I am [action] said [name].

I am	⬜	said	⬜
_____ _____		_____ _____	

➡ Use any computer program with the facility *Pen* to model the writing process. With PowerPoint, make slides of repetitive sentences. Have the children watch you make the sentences; then have them read them and, later, with your support, write sentences on the slides using *Pen*.

- Set the screen **Blank presentation**
  New slide
  Choose an **Auto layout—(title only)** ☐
  Font **Comic Sans MS 40**

- Type in front of the children: **Here is a dog.** [double spacing]

- After writing the phrase, highlight it, click **Custom anima-tion—effects, wipe right** or **appear.**

- Click **Slide show** and **mouse.** The text will appear. Click △ the icon in the lower left-hand corner of your screen and then **Pen.** Using the mouse, you can draw a dog on the slide to match your phrase.

- Continue making slides. Click on **Insert,** then **new slide** and follow the above instructions beginning at "set the screen." Next slide could be: **Here is a girl.**

Pen markings erase when each slide is closed. You can revisit the slides using *Pen*—for example:

- Children draw the nouns.

- Children rewrite the phrase under the original phrase.

- Substitute other words for the word *a* or *Here.* For example, write *the* or *This* . . . and write the new phrases underneath the original.

- Add to the phrase: "Here is a dog," *said Melanie.*

Have on file a collection of digital photographs or children's drawings you have scanned. When you want to begin with a photo-graph or a drawing, click **Insert: picture from file** or **from scanner,** then type the phrase to match the picture.

You could print copies for the children to take home to read. (This is a quick way to make books for the children to read.)

➵ Read a big book or poem for a week that has repetitive phrases and adapt the text. For example, using the big book *The Tram Ride* (or a similar one), you could change the nouns on the first page:

Instead of "A turtle got on the tram," the children may suggest "A crab got on the bus" or "A snake got on the bus."

Figure 1a.

Figure 1b.

➡ Refer to the initial letter of each day on the alphabet chart and introduce alliteration. In front of the children, write a poem in which the words following the day name begin with the same initial sound as that of the day. Once the children have the idea, they can suggest animals with the same beginning letter.

Monday, mad monkey

Tuesday, terrible turtle

Wednesday, wobbly worm

➡ Have the children take turns telling their news. Write a child's news in a large "class news" book. Try to link words to previously made books.

Last night mom made spaghetti. E.P. [child's initials]

Model writing the news. Point out familiar initial letters, ask them to listen for sounds they can hear, make analogies with words they know (for example, *can, ran*), and help them investigate words.

➡ Make a big book based on a topic—for example, "food":

I like ＿＿＿＿＿＿＿＿ and ＿＿＿＿＿＿＿＿ .

I like ＿＿＿＿＿＿＿＿ said ＿＿＿＿＿＿＿＿ .

➡ Get the children to cut out magazine pictures of animals or vehicles. Model using them in a sentence:

Here is a [car].

➡ Make sentence labels with the children and introduce words and their beginning sounds. Make labels of frequently used words to place around the classroom.

This is a window.   Here is a chair.

We can look out of it.   You can sit on it.

Later you could add: **and** . . .

➥ To reinforce the concept of "word" as distinct from "letters,"
make word poem mobiles. Explain to the children how words are
made by putting letters together. Have a magnetic board and letters
and show how to put selected words from a rhyme together, using left-
to-right movement, sequencing, and one-on-one matching of each
word and the sound each word makes. Make one or two mobiles with
words written on separate cards.

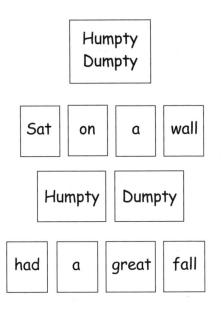

Independent Writing

After shared writing, children should write independently. There may
be a big variation in what children represent as writing—pictures,
letterlike shapes, random letters, initial letters, and invented spelling.
Praise their efforts. At this stage children need to take risks. If possible, it is great for children to have a set of plastic letters on their desk
with which to make new words before they write them. Certainly, an
alphabet chart on the desk is a great reference.

➤ Children love making their own little books. When children make their own books, they are actively using writing and spelling techniques they have learned during the shared sessions. You have already constructed many phrases and words in front of the children, and now they will write their own phrases. Folding a piece of 8½" by 11" paper in half will create a four page book. Make lots of little blank books—some could be cut into shapes. Lead a shared-writing session relating to the books the children are about to make. Have the children try to write before you help them. Ask them to try to write the phrase you have been modeling—at least the first letters of the words. Remind them about listening for the first sound. You can direct them to look at an alphabet chart and make a link with the sound, picture, or symbol—for example, sound /d/, picture of a duck, the letter *d*. Some topics children could write about are:

Me

My name is _____ [I like to] _____	[I can] _____

My family and me

[This is me] _____	[This is my] _____

My pet

[I can see my] _____	[It is] _____

Figure 2.

➥ Read a story to the children and have them recount a sentence (or more) about what happened.

➥ Show a picture, or enact a story using puppets, or felt characters, and ask children to tell the story before they attempt to write it.

Handwriting

When children write, they can only concentrate on spelling if they are fluent handwriters. For some children, discriminating between letters, knowing where to begin a letter, and deciding what direction to go after that is often a mystery, and this can inhibit a child's spelling progress. In the early days of a child's education, handwriting lessons should be implemented daily and done briskly for short periods—approximately fifteen minutes.

Children use three senses when handwriting: sight, hearing, and touch (which is manifested in their hand movements). You need to support the children by getting them to attend to the look of the letter, establish the direction of the letter, determine where to start and where to go next, and make symbol and sound connections.

Select a group of children's work each week that represents the letter studied, and introduce new letters by linking them to known letters.

"The *h* begins at the top like the *l* and goes down, making a stick. . . . "

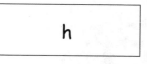

Choose groups of letters that go in the same direction. It helps to begin with top-to-bottom letters, such as *l*, *h*, and then when these are secure move to counterclockwise letters, such as *c* and *o*.

Have the children learn to write these letters by practicing them in their spelling books using "look; say and write; cover and write; check" (see Individual Spelling, p. 38).

➥ Read big books, poems, rhymes, alphabet books, and songs that contain the featured letter at the beginning of words.

Concentrate on one letter each week   After the reading, sit the children in a circle. Be sure each child has a white- or blackboard, and markers or chalk. Join in the circle with the same writing tools in front of you.

Figure 3.

➼ Begin by modeling the letter and reciting the movement of
the letter. For example, for the letter *l*—"Begin at the top and
move your pencil down." Get the children to verbalize the letter
sound or name while writing on their boards and in their books.
When children are at their desks writing, encourage them to develop the correct pencil grip, hold the book with their other hand,
and sit with their backs against their chairs.

An example of a week-long handwriting program for the letter l.

➼ Each day, sit in a circle with the children and model the
letter *l* on your white- or blackboard. As you do so, say the
sound of the letter. Have the children write in the air, on a
partner's back, on the floor, and then on the small white- or
blackboards. As they write on the boards, ask them to verbalize *l*
or sing a song that features the letter for that week—for example
Lucy Lion l l l. After a few days of practicing the letter, model a
few words that begin with the letter *l*, such as *like* or *lips.* You
can write the first letter in a color different from the rest of the

word. When the children have finished writing their letters on their boards they can move on to various activities to reinforce what they have learned. For example:

■ Make an 8½" by 11" jigsaw letter.

■ Find the hidden *l*s in the picture.

■ Make a sheet with a letter and a word to write. Put that word into a sentence—for example, "I like lips."

```
I _____

           lips

      _____

  I like lips.

      _____
```

Reinforcement Activities

Left-to-Right Directionality

➤ Have strips of cards with a shape outlined in green at the left end. Ask the children to begin here and place shapes along the card. They can develop a pattern, but this is not necessary as the focus is left-to-right movement.

➤ Have children, using left-to-right movement, draw different-colored ribbons blowing from a circle.

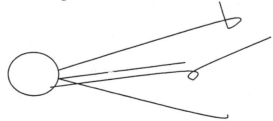

"Hearing" Games

➥ Explain that each letter has its own name and sound by using the initial letter or sound of children's names: "What does Anna begin with . . . ?" Bring to the children's attention that although some children's names begin with the same letter, some letters have more than one sound.

➥ Play "hearing" games in which the children listen for letters that sound the same.

Make a set of cards—half blue (same) and half red (different). Give a card of each color to each child in the class and tell the children what each card means: blue is for the same letter sound and red is for a different letter sound. For example, *l, m* (children hold up a red card); *n, o* (children hold up a red card); and *p, p* (children hold up a blue card).

Then ask the children to listen to words that have the same or different initial sounds. Say two words and ask the children to hold up a blue card (same) if the words begin with the same initial sound and a red card (different) if the words begin with different initial sounds. You can extend this game by saying initial blends or rhyming patterns. (Carefully evaluate children who look at another child's card; they may be having difficulty discriminating sounds.)

➥ Recite "hearing" poems and ask children what sound they heard at the beginning of the onomatopoeic words.

Listen to the birds
Tweet, tweet
What sound do these words begin with?

Listen to the lion
Roar, roar
What sound do these words begin with?

Listen to the bees
Buzz, buzz
What sound do these words begin with?

Listen to the wind
Whoo, whoo

What sound do these words begin with?

➻ Play "I hear, with my little ear, a word that begins with /p/ [or other selected sound] and starts like *Paul* [or other selected word]."

Sound and Symbol Relationship and Fluency

▪ Have the children assemble a variety of alphabet jigsaws.

▪ Have the children make alphabet books.

▪ With partners, have the children shape their bodies into letter shapes.

▪ Play a guessing game: "What letter is it?"

▪ Set up a table with things beginning with a particular letter. Have the children touch each item and name it.

▪ Have a "feely" box that children reach into and identify the letters by feeling their shapes.

Categorizing Letters

➻ Place a selection of magnetic letters on the left-hand side of the magnetic board and show children how to quickly group them into different categories—for example: *similar, different, sticks, circles, hooks, b's, d's.* Ask the children to find the type of letters you designate and quickly group them on the right side of the board.

➻ Play "Find My Letter." A child chooses a letter from a box of letters and the class asks questions to find out what letter the child has. Questions could be "Is it a stick letter?" or "Does it go around counterclockwise?" or "Is it like a curly *c*?" or "Is it an *o*?"

Initial Letter

➻ Have cards that state:

Find as many
items as you
can starting
with *d.*

➥ Make large letters—for example:

c d e

On cards, write words beginning with the focus letters. Children sort the words by placing *c* words in the large *c*, *d* words in the large *d*, *e* words in the large *e*.

➥ Develop the idea that lots of words start with the same letter. Play "I spy"; place various items on a shelf or a table, and tell children that is where they should look to think of "I spy" items.

Hearing Sounds in Words

➥ As children are writing, teach them how to listen for sounds. Draw boxes (no more than four). As the children say the word slowly, write or place letters (plastic or cards) in the boxes. Ask, "What sound did you hear first . . . next . . . last?"

c	a	t

Letter Sequence in Words

➥ Give children plastic letters to match under a word written in large print on a card.

come

➥ To help the children realize that words are made up of differing numbers of letters (two, three, or more), make folding names. Choose two children's names, a short name and a long name. Write the names (Anna and Christopher, for example) on separate cards and fold the cards after each letter. Unfold the cards and show that words are different lengths. Repeat this other days, writing other children's names with contrasting word lengths.

Practice Letter Writing

➥ Ask the children to practice writing one or two letters (or words) each day using different mediums. For example:

- Write on paper.
- Rainbow a letter or word with crayons (follow the shape of the letter).
- Write in sand.
- Write on a chair with a finger.
- Write on a white- or blackboard.
- Use play dough to make letters.
- Paint large letters and words.
- Make words using matchsticks.
- Write on a Magna Doodle®.

Make a HUGE *m* outside on the asphalt. Ask children to walk on the line and recite, "m—begin at the top, go down, back up and around, back up and around."

➥ Introduce finger strengthening activities such as threading beads.

Assessment

At the beginning of and periodically throughout the year, assess children's letter fluency and record their progress. You could use the letter assessment grid on p. 33, on which the children write the letters alongside the pictures. Before having children do the assessment, "read" the pictures together a few times. Children should recognize and write the letters quickly. The assessment can be a class task. It may be that some children will require individual coaching on some of the pictures. Say what the picture is and ask, "What does _____ begin with?"

Some children will know all the letters you have taught, some will know more than you have taught, and some will know almost all of the letters. Children who are not learning any letters will need special assistance individually or in small groups.

Assessment **WRITE THE FIRST LETTER**

Name: **Date:**

Figure 2.1: *Black Line Master: Letter Assessment*

Keep a record of children's developing letter knowledge. Check off (✔) each letter when a child knows the letter. At a quick glance, you will see a child's progress over the seasons.

Letter Knowledge Record

Name _____ **Year** _____

Beginning (Fall) Date _____ **Baseline** **Total**

Recognition a b c d e f g h i j k l m n o p q r s t u v w x y z

Written Orientation a b c d e f g h i j k l m n o p q r s t u v w x y z

Difficulties

Figure 2.2: *Black Line Master: Letter Knowledge Record (detail)*

Classroom Strategies for Word Spellers

As children are learning to spell words they are also learning strategies to help them analyze and frame mental images of words for future recall. These strategies include:

- Examining a word for precise information—for example, the beginning letter, a digraph or small word within a word, medial vowels.
- Using analogy to get to new words from those already known (linking known words that share common patterns). For example, words that rhyme share common patterns. If a child knows how to spell *pop*, and the new word is *shop*, you can ask "Have you seen a word like *shop* before?"
- Saying the word slowly and listening for sound sequences. By using this method, a child learns distinctive features of letters, letter clusters, and letter order (Clay 1993). For example:

w e n t   h is   sh e

- Working on large units rather than single letters (single-letter analysis is slow; there is more to learn, and therefore more error can occur). Patterns of letters become recognizable in groups—for example, initial blends, digraphs, rhymes, visual patterns, smaller words within words, syllables, compound words.
- Getting phonological information from several levels of language—identities for letters, digraphs, blends, syllables.
- Using alternatives—for example, long or short vowel sounds (p*a*n versus p*a*ne).

Shared Reading

Big Books and Poems

Teaching focuses could include unusual letter sounds (*c* making the *s* sound), blends, digraphs, rhymes, visual patterns (*night, sight*), syllables, smaller words within words, capitalization, and punctuation. Decide what your teaching focus will be, and choose a big book or poem that models this focus. Get children to suggest problem-solving strategies. Plan reinforcement activities to secure knowledge about words.

➡ In the big book *Angus Thought He Was Big* the teaching focus is the consonant *c* making the *s* sound: *circus, city, Alice, space.* Read the book, have students make predictions, and discuss the story. Then, over a period of time, study the spelling focus—**c** as **s** sound—and add more words to a word list. Play class and small-group games to reinforce this unusual spelling.

➥ The nursery rhyme "Jack and Jill" has many high frequency words. Write the rhyme in large print:

Jack and Jill went up the hill

To fetch a pail of water.

Jack fell down and broke his crown

And Jill came tumbling after.

On separate cards, write the high frequency words from the rhyme. Match the cards and talk about features of the words—for example, what a particular word begins with. Build up a class word display and place it where it can be easily accessed by all the children. Each day, direct the children to the display to talk about or locate words needed for written tasks. You do not have to write every word; one example of a pattern will allow you to model how the children can hear and see patterns through analogy. For example, once *went* is written on the display, a child who needs to know how to spell *sent* can refer to the rhyming pattern at the end of *went*.

Aa		Ww		th	
a		went		the	
and					

Chart

➥ When modeling writing and during individual conferences, show the children how to help themselves by silently asking questions as they write and practice their spelling. The question map (see p. 39), itemizes strategies they can use. Also put a spelling question map at the beginning of their spelling books. Gradually introduce the questions. After a while ask, "How are you going to think about the word?" A question map allows children to make informed attempts at spelling. Keep revising the questions associated with particular spelling strategies. Have children tell you the strategies they used to problem-solve a word.

Writing

Shared writing (including guided writing with small groups) should emphasize the structures of written genres, the languages, and words associated with different written genres. For example, in procedures, recounts, and narratives, ideas are linked by using sequencing adjectives (*first, next, last*) and adverbs (*after, later, then, finally*). When children write reports they learn to spell new technical words and to use subordinate conjunctions (*as, because*), and limiting adjectives (*most, some*). When they write an exposition (argument), they use modal verbs (*might, may*), contrasting conjunctions (*but, yet*), and conjunctive adverbs (*also, in addition, however*).

An interesting study by Olivia O'Sullivan in the United Kingdom Reading Association journal *Reading* found, "As children wrote widely and at increasing length, their spelling noticeably developed. In the case of all children, the experience of writing in different genres widened their written vocabulary and therefore the range of words they were attempting to spell."

Individual Spelling

Don Holdaway's comment "Knowing some two hundred [basic sight] words gives immediate access to 30–40 percent of running English," suggests that children should quickly learn to spell a large number of high frequency words correctly. Once they do, their attention is not on spelling but on the content of their written pieces.

High frequency words are words that recur often in early writing and reading. Children are generally all over the place in their ability to write these words correctly. An individual high frequency word spelling program increases correctly written vocabulary at a level and pace that suits each child. Discuss strategies with children as words are placed into spelling books—for example, linking w*ere* with h*er*; saying words slowly so every sound can be heard (*w e n t*); looking at the

Questions I ask myself when I learn to spell

- What does the word *mean*?

- What does the word *begin* with?

- What does the word *end* with?

- What can I hear and see in the *middle*?

- What *large units* can I hear and see?   Rhymes

Syllables	Suffixes (ed, ing)
Prefixes (un, dis)	Blends (bl, st)
Digraphs (th, ar)	Compounds

- Does the word *look like any other word*?

- Are there *double letters*?

- What is the *small word* in the word?

- Have I tried *saying the word slowly*?

- Have I looked closely at the *tricky parts* (ough)?

small words (*before*); thinking about tricky parts (bec*au*se); and breaking long words into syllables (*to/geth/er*). Encourage each child to take responsibility for his or her own learning of spelling (the "look, cover, write, check" process) and focus on particular strategies.

Children who use a variety of strategies, practice new words thoroughly, and can spell the words correctly more than once orally generally retain the correct spelling when writing.

Test for Unknown Words and Maintain a Record Sheet

➼ Maintain a list of high frequency words and an identical record sheet for each child. (See the example below—the Black Line Masters include lists of 240 high frequency words.) Keep all the children's record sheets in a box for easy access. In conferences, discuss a few aspects of the child's written piece (for example, the ideas and language), identifying the strategies the child has used to spell words and have the child spell words orally.

HIGH FREQUENCY SPELLING RECORD SHEET				
Name: ⟶ Focus:				
the	I	is	a	to
am	my	we	in	of
and	it	here	on	went
like	he	up	go	are
going	me	can	this	look

Test the children by reading the words across the columns to the class or a group and have the children write the words. At the end of this exercise, collect the sheets and on each child's record sheet mark a check (✔) for known words and leave unknown words blank.

Known and Unknown Words

➡ Record unknown words in children's spelling books. Mark these words with an *S* in the child's record sheet. Give each child a certain number of words (one to four) to learn to spell. Below is an example of a child's record sheet with:

- ▪ Known words marked with a (✔).
- ▪ Unknown words blank.
- ▪ Unknown words placed into spelling book marked *S*.

Name		Focus: • what words mean • what word begins with • making analogies			
S the	 and	✔ I	✔ a	✔ to	 was
S it	 we	 in	 of	 he	 my

Practice New Words

➡ Stress that to be able to spell words, it is necessary to be able to read them. Give children who have reading difficulties a buddy to read the word just for them.

Teach children to look at the word, say the word slowly as they write it, close their eyes to picture the word, and "cover, write, and check." Have them write the word three times, looking carefully at the example you have written in their spelling books, and at the same time ask themselves questions—for example, "What is the tricky part?" After they have said the word slowly while writing it, ask them to close their eyes and see it "in their head." Have them cover the word and write it a fourth time. Then ask them to check to see whether their spelling is correct. Words on the first page (and following pages) of their spelling books could look like this:

(look/write)				(cover/write)
a n d	and	and	and	and
the	the	the	the	the
a	a	a	a	a
I	I	I	I	I

For selected words, divide the letters and sounds into boxes and have the children say the words slowly, listening for each sound. Give the children this card to remind them of the procedure.

> 1. *Look* at the word.
> 2. As you *write* the word 3 times, say the word slowly.
> 3. *Cover* the word and *write* it.
> 4. *Check.* Have you written the word correctly?

Practice Old Words

Until a word is checked off three times (see the next activity), have the children rehearse their words each day. Ask them to read the word, close their books, mentally spell the word, then open their books and check.

Test Practiced Words

➥ During conferences, test children's ability to read and spell the words in their spelling books. First ask them to read the word; then have them close the spelling book and ask them to spell the word orally. If they do both correctly, check (✔) the word in their spelling books. When they receive three checks over a period of time, cross out the word and assume it is known. As your spelling program progresses and children spell their words correctly during conferences, their spelling-book pages will look like this:

(look/write)			(cover/write)	
✔✔✔ and	*and*	*and*	*and*	*and*
the	*the*	*the*	*the*	*the*
✔✔✔ can	*can*	*can*	*can*	*can*
✔✔ cake	*cake*	*cake*	*cake*	*cake*
✔ was	*was*	*was*	*was*	*was*

Figure 4.

➼ Take words from children's independent writing (genres) and study themes and list them in their spelling books.

➼ When children are learning letters, place the unknown letters in their spelling books.

Reinforcement Activities

Look at the Final Letter, Initial Letters

➼ Play Word Stairs with a group or the whole class. In this game, a child writes the first word on the top step. The next child looks at the ending letter and writes a word beginning with that letter on the step below. Children take turns and continue down the "staircase," each time using the last letter in the previous word to begin the new word.

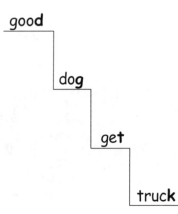

Look at Words

➼ Each day, show two spellings of a word and ask, "What looks right?"

becos   or   because?

➼ Play Word Stairs with groups of older students. In this variation, a child writes a word on the top step. The next child retains the first two letters of the word and makes a new word on the step below by changing the ending group of letters. Children can use dictionaries to find words.

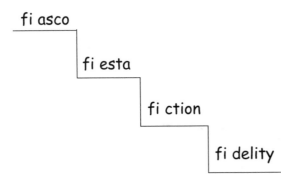

fi asco
fi esta
fi ction
fi delity

Search for the Beginning, Ending, and Medial Vowel or Medial Consonant

➡ Make new words with magnetic letters:

Change the beginning consonant: <u>b</u>at
                                  <u>h</u>at
Change the ending consonant: ma<u>n</u>
                                  ma<u>t</u>
Change the medial consonant: ma<u>d</u>e   ma<u>k</u>e
Change the medial vowel: r<u>a</u>n   r<u>u</u>n

➡ Play Change the Word with a friend. Begin with a word from your latest reading. Choose two consecutive letters to become the initial letters of a new word.

For example: spe<u>ak</u>
               <u>ak</u>in
               <u>ki</u>nd
               <u>in</u>stead

Search for Smaller Words in Words

➡ Read the letters of a word from left to right and make as many words as you can.

Christmas	yourself	landmark	pineapple
Chris	you	an	pin
is	your	and	in

Christ	our	mark	pine
as	self	ark	apple
	elf		

Search for Beginning, Medial, and Ending Digraphs

➥ Play Word Sorts, sorting the words by digraph placement: beginning, medial, and ending.

<u>or</u>der	w<u>or</u>ld	doct<u>or</u>	f<u>or</u>
<u>sh</u>ow	wi<u>sh</u>es	wa<u>sh</u>	
<u>th</u>ey	mo<u>th</u>er	mo<u>th</u>	
<u>ar</u>ticle	c<u>ar</u>t	st<u>ar</u>	

Search for Visual Patterns

➥ Write words that have unusual patterns on cards. Have the children sort the words according to matching patterns.

ate	ight	ough
plate	night	through
mate	sight	thought
late	slight	rough

Search for Words

➥ Write a number of words without leaving spaces between them and have children find the individual words:

cowwherefactsover   or   playdaystayray

Listen for Rhyming Pairs and Alliteration

➥ Write words taken from a poem or a story on cards. The two players each sit behind a barrier or sit back-to-back. One child has the set of cards and says each word. The other child responds orally with a rhyming word or a word beginning with the same sound. (For the older children, increase the complexity of the words.)

Be Aware of Beginning Blends or Ending Rhymes

➥ Make as many words as you can using initial blends (the words must make sense):

br *(brain, broad, brush)*

st *(station, stocking, stole)*

➥ Make as many words as you can using rhymes (the words must make sense):

ack *(slack, back, rack)*

old *(hold, mold, bold)*

Work on Large Units

Visualizing clusters of letters—syllables, words within words, compound words, initial blends, rhymes, digraphs, prefixes, suffixes, or other visual patterns—is a strategy children use when spelling.

➥ Make word jigsaw puzzles. Cut words into segments that you want to bring to the children's attention:

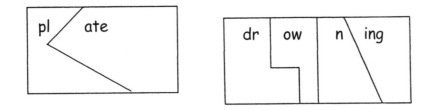

Use Analogy to Get to New Words

➥ Begin with a word and have children change one letter at a time to make new words:

car   cat   cut   put   pub   rub   rob

Anticipate Words

➻ Play What's the Word? Begin each day by writing the initial letter of a word, followed by dashes indicating the rest of the letters, on the board; have the children discover the word (or one with the same number of letters) by anticipating what the next letters will be. (For the older children, increase the complexity of the words.)

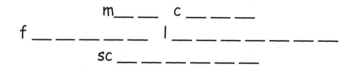

Reinforce Initial Blends, Digraphs, and Initial Letters

➻ Play Tic Tac Toe. Make lots of blank grids.

Have each child choose a pattern, letter, or sound he or she is going to use. Player A, for example, chooses words beginning with the letters *th* and player B chooses words beginning with the letter *c*. Each player, in turn, tries to write three words consecutively, horizontally, vertically, or diagonally.

come	the	think
that	then	clear
care	cannot	three

Try again!

Reinforce Ending Rhymes and Suffixes

➥ Have children create "What is . . . " and "Who is . . . " spelling problems for their peers to solve. Child A writes a noun on a piece of paper and asks a *what* or *who* question relating to the noun. The rest of the class writes short sentences answering the question. For example:

What is tall?   Who is jumping?

A giraffe is tall.   A kangaroo is jumping.

A building is tall.   A girl is jumping.

A giant is tall.   *A dog is jumping.*

Use a Combination of Strategies

➥ List between three and six clearly spaced words on a card. Have the children look at the words and work out ways to remember the spelling of each word. After a given time, cover the list and have the children write the words. (This could be a team game or a partner game. For the older children, increase the complexity of the words.)

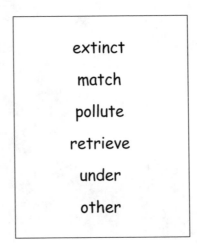

extinct

match

pollute

retrieve

under

other

➼ Play Making Sandwiches (class circle game). (There are twenty six letters in the alphabet—if you have more children than that in the class the extras can wear vowel sounds; if you have fewer, some children can wear cards on their backs and fronts.) Write the consonants in one color and the vowels in another color. Attach string to each letter card so it can be worn around the neck. To play the game, one child calls out a word and the children with the letters of the word step out of the circle and

Figure 5a.

Figure 5b.

come together to form the word. If there are double letters and not enough children, the child with that letter moves to different positions to indicate its multiple use in the word.

➤ Play Spelling Stumpers (a class game). Ask a child to think of a word with an unusual spelling—for example, *rhyme*. One by one, children spell the word *rhyme* as you record each spelling on the board. When the word is recognized as being correctly spelled, stop. You can emphasize all sorts of strategies the children can use when problem-solving the word. Finally, have the children, individually or in groups, look up the meaning of the word in a dictionary.

Figure 6.

➦ Play Bingo. Have in mind particular things you want to reinforce—high frequency words, rhymes, visual patterns, initial blends, digraphs, suffixes, prefixes. Make boards and matching cards.

train	mate	play		play
frame	strain	ache		strain

Using the cards, one child says the words, one at a time. The players respond by placing markers on matching words on their boards. The first player to cover all the words on his or her board with markers yells "Bingo!"

➦ For a quick end-of-day activity, write parts of words on the board. Put children into teams of four and have the children quickly fill in the missing parts. (For the older children, increase the complexity of the words.)

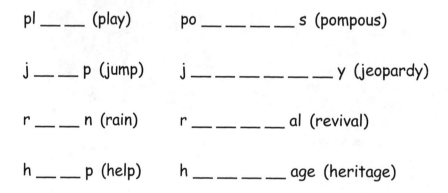

pl __ __ (play)   po __ __ __ __ s (pompous)

j __ __ p (jump)   j __ __ __ __ __ __ y (jeopardy)

r __ __ n (rain)   r __ __ __ __ al (revival)

h __ __ p (help)   h __ __ __ __ age (heritage)

Practice

➦ Have children practice spelling their words using the Kid Pix Studio computer program. When the screen displays the **Kid Pix Studio Picker:**
- Choose **Kid Pix**
- Click the pencil icon

Using the mouse, the children can then write words from their spelling books or dictionaries. It's a stimulating way for children to practice spelling!

Assessment

The aim of assessing any spelling program is to:

- ■ Analyze errors so that specific problems can be addressed.
- ■ Gauge whether the child is at an appropriate spelling level.
- ■ Gauge whether the words learned during modeled, focused, and individual spelling programs are being carried over into children's writing.

Spelling fluency is evident within the context of continuous writing. Analyze children's spelling in continuous writing—an assignment or a sentence or story purposely composed for assessment purposes.

Regular Assignments

Examining spelling within a piece of writing lets you see how children are tackling spelling as they write. You could examine a variety of the groups' written pieces at different times. If you ask children to generate specific samples for analytical purposes, provide the very best conditions—uninterrupted quiet—for the children to write.

Purposely Composed Stories or Sentences

Write a short story or series of sentences containing the applicable words (for example, high frequency words learned during the term). Have everyone take the list of words home to learn.

Dictate the story or sentences for children to write.

Analyzing a Child's Spelling

Words spelled correctly or incorrectly tell you what to teach next—what knowledge and strategies children are using or not using when they attempt to spell words. For example:

- ■ Does their spelling match normally occurring developmental stages?

■ Is their spelling unpredictable (guessing), or are they confusing letter sequences?

■ Are they relying on phonological information? Are they consistently and correctly writing the first, last, and medial sounds of words?

■ Are they able to systematically visualize and internalize letter sequences and structures of words, as well as mentally store and retrieve them? Do they distinguish between meanings of homophones (for example *site, sight*)?

Analysis should be part of any spelling assessment, and you could consider the overall percentage of errors.

SPELLING ERROR ANALYSIS (EXAMPLE)			
Name _____		Date _____	
Child's spelling	Text spelling	Analysis	Analysis
dout	boat	Sound - initial - medial ✔ - ending ✔	Visual - initial <u>d/b</u> confusion - medial <u>ou/oa</u> confusion - ending
withe	which	Sound - initial ✔ - medial ✔ - ending	Visual - initial - medial - ending

Use **Black Line Master: Spelling Error Analysis** to record your analysis.

Classroom Strategies for Language Spellers

Conventional spellers use a wide range of strategies that vary with the word and the speller's previous experiences related to the word. Children eventually have the ability to visualize letter sequences in words, as well as mentally store and retrieve these sequences. They become confident strategic problem solvers.

Their attention now is focused on the study of word forms (words associated with grammatical structures)—on how word forms are used within language structures (syntax). Children learn that to maintain meaning and correct sentence structures they must know what verb form to use, whether to use the plural or singular form, and what suffixes (endings) to use to change verbs into nouns—for example *manage* (verb) and *management* (noun). They learn when to use adjectives and adverbs, and when to add an apostrophe—before or after the **s**. Understanding basic spelling principles such as doubling consonants and changing the final **y** to **i** before adding any suffix, except **ing**, extends children's knowledge and develops spelling fluency and the use of more formal language when they write.

Focused shared reading reinforces learning about particular word forms and language structures within the context of continuous print. Language spellers are also challenged to think independently about word forms and language structures. After reading a novel or an article, for example, fluent readers can respond to tasks that involve divergent thinking, like those Edward de Bono advocates in his book *Six Thinking Hats*. They can also research origins of words, homophones, and how suffixes can change word forms.

The more experienced and knowledgeable children are about words, the more able they are to proofread their writing—identifying possible spelling and grammatical errors and either correcting them themselves or consulting dictionaries. Shared and individual writing are the natural contexts in which language spellers habitually use and demonstrate proofreading and self-correction processes.

**GUIDING STRATEGIC SPELLING FOR
LANGUAGE SPELLERS:**

Written models:

 Shared reading.

 Independent reading.

 Shared writing (to include guided writing), proofreading.

Opportunities for practice and feedback:

 Writing, proofreading.

 Reinforcement activities.

 Assessment, writing analysis.

Shared Reading

Big-Book Fiction, Nonfiction, Poems, and Articles

Big print is an essential teaching resource in elementary classrooms. During shared reading of enlarged print (don't forget overhead projectors or large print on computer screens), the teacher and children work according to a purposeful plan focusing on particular teaching and learning points. Shared reading is for the whole class.

When choosing material for shared reading, have a particular word form focus in mind and use examples in the book (which must be *clear*) to point out how the word form is used within a particular language structure. You may cater to a particular group in your class, or the focus may be a universal learning point.

Antonym	the opposite of another word
Synonym	a word that has a similar meaning to another word (writers want to avoid overusing the same word)
Suffixes	word parts added to the ends of words
Prefixes	word parts added to the beginning of words
Homonyms	make connections between spelling and meaning - homographs—words that are spelled the same but have different meanings - homophones—words that are pronounced the same but have different spellings and meanings
Verbs	action (*walk*), linking (*is*), auxilary (*might*); except for commands, verbs have a subject (noun or pronoun); the tenses are past, present, future, and auxiliary; there are four forms—base form (*talk, grow*), third person present singular (*he talks, it grows*), past tense (*talked, grew*), and the past participle (*talked, grown*)
Adverbs	place, time, or manner; words used to say where, when, or how about a verb
Adjectives	give more information about a noun; factual (*red*), opinion (*silly*), quantity (*four*), and classifier (*collie dog*); the classifiers are the basic word (*strong*), the comparative (*stronger*), and the superlative (*strongest*)
Pronouns	personal (1st person [*I*], 2nd person [*you*], 3rd person [*he*], and possessive [*mine, yours*])
Collective nouns	groups considered as units: e.g., *assembly, bunch, collection, drawers*
Singular/Plural	*girl girls man men*
Conjunctions	make compound and complex sentences; place (*where*), time (*after*), manner (*as*), or cause (*because*)
Derivations	English words derived from other languages (etymology)
Idioms, slang colloquialisms	people's language
Apostrophe	contraction (missing letter) or possessive
Capitals	used at the beginning of sentences, for proper names and titles, or in acronyms

Possible word form focuses

FOCUSED SHARED READING – A WEEKLY PLAN

Big book title: *Failed Again*   **Prior knowledge:** *none*

Focus: First learning about adverbs—they modify verbs (tell how, when, or where something is done).

Follow-up activity: Verb and adverb cards used in a variety of ways

Monday: Knowing the story

Predict—draw attention to the title and the illustration on the cover and ask what it might mean.

Try to capture the anticipation of something about to happen. What is going to happen to the character? Can the children predict the ending? Write suggested endings on paper before reading the ending.

Tuesday: The language focus

Retell part, Reread part

Ask or explain what an adverb is. Isolate the example adverb (*hardly*) written before the verb (*wait*) in the text and see if children can find others (*definitely, really*) written before the verbs (*looking, going*). What is common about these adverbs is that they end in *ly*.

List three adverbs from the text on a sheet of paper.

Wednesday: Developing the language focus

Retell, Reread

Ask children what an adverb is.

Look at the adverbs listed on the large sheet. Can the children think of other adverbs ending in *ly*? List three to four adverbs. Write a sentence and see how the adverb fits into the structure of the sentence. Where is the verb?

Thursday: Further developing the language focus

Retell, Reread

Class circle activity: Have adverbs and verbs written on cards. Give verb and adverb cards to children and let them find a match to orally structure a verb-adverb sentence.

Adverbs—terribly, nobly, forcibly, simply, visibly, noticeably, feebly, comfortably, probably, idly, solely

Friday: Rereading with minimum interruption and maximum expression and enjoyment

Class circle activity from Thursday.

Revisit the verb and adverb cards as a language activity—write and sort sentences; find other adverbs in the dictionary.

➤ Once a teaching focus has been decided, choose a big book that has at least a few good examples of the particular word form. Plan a program for a week (see sample, p. 58)—for example, reading the book every day, searching for examples of the learning focus, putting that focus into other contexts, and assigning an activity or independent task that reinforces the focus.

Independent Reading

Children who are reading a novel, an article, nonfiction, or newspapers for the purpose of completing a book review, research, or written argument about an issue can also use de Bono's **"Thinking Hats"** to extend their knowledge about word forms. (Make the hats attractive to look at—for example, put glitter around the edges.) Devise tasks that encourage divergent thinking about word forms. The children need to be well versed in word forms such as adjectives, adverbs, and suffixes before they undertake this independent work.

➤ Make a collection of "thinking hats" assigning general word form tasks for children to do. Each of de Bono's hats defines a certain type of thinking:

Red	words that stimulate feelings
Black	tricky words—problems, what goes wrong
Yellow	good strategies—things that work
White	facts
Green	creative solutions—new or further ideas
Blue	plan/review—strategies to use/what worked

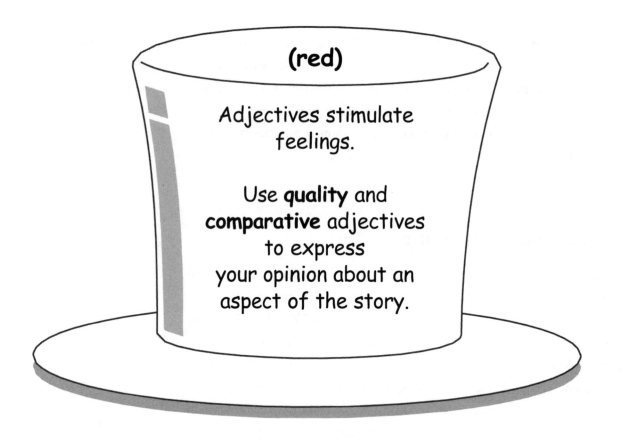

(red)

Adjectives stimulate feelings.

Use **quality** and **comparative** adjectives to express your opinion about an aspect of the story.

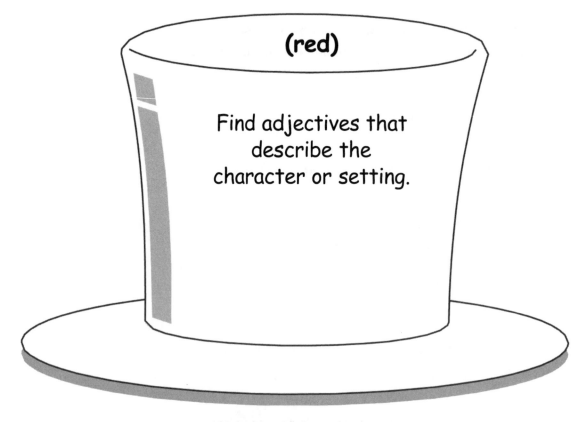

(red)

Find adjectives that describe the character or setting.

(red)

Find three nouns in your latest reading and find at least three adjectives to describe each noun.

For example, *pear: yellow, smooth, balloon-shaped*

(black)

Some word forms are tricky.

Find three irregular past tense verbs in your latest reading.

Write an acrostic poem using the verbs.

For example: r_____
o_____
d_____
e_____

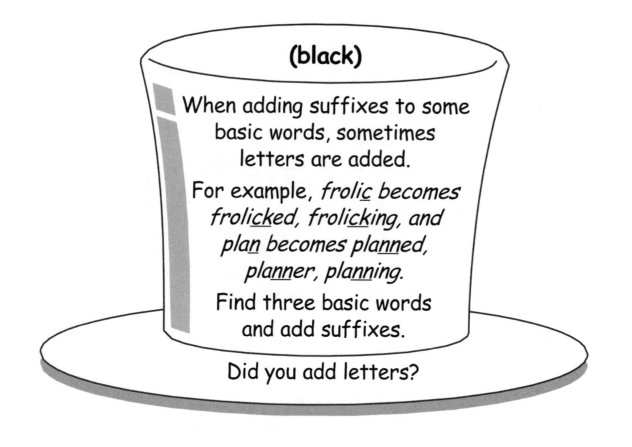

(black)

When adding suffixes to some basic words, sometimes letters are added.

For example, *frolic becomes frolicked, frolicking, and plan becomes planned, planner, planning.*

Find three basic words and add suffixes.

Did you add letters?

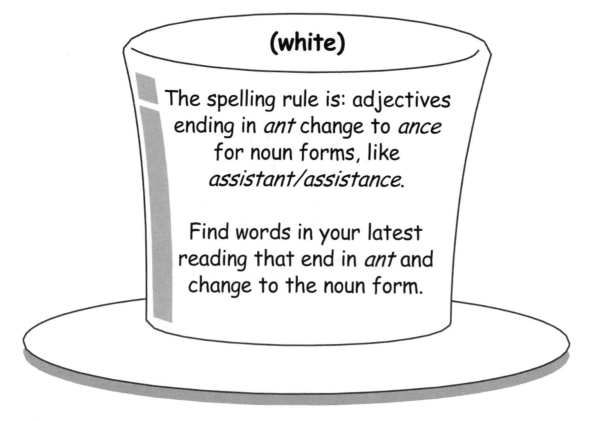

(white)

The spelling rule is: adjectives ending in *ant* change to *ance* for noun forms, like *assistant/assistance.*

Find words in your latest reading that end in *ant* and change to the noun form.

(white)

An adverb is used to say when, how, or where about a verb— for example, how the character moved (walked *slowly*).

Find one *where* and *how* adverb in your latest reading and write a sentence using it.

(yellow)

Write down homophones as you find them in your latest reading.

Draw pictures of them, give the pictures to a partner, and let your partner work out the homophones.

(yellow)

There are words you know the meaning of and how to spell.

Find a word in your latest reading that begins with a prefix or ends in a suffix and play the game T-Junction with a partner.

For example: *dis*appear
o
i
need*less*
t

(yellow)

Make a Concentration game using
conjunctions you find
in your latest reading.

Make two matching cards
for each conjunction.

Play the game with a friend.

(green)

Be creative with words.

Look for words in your latest
reading for which you
can create opposite meanings.

Rewrite the sentences
using these antonyms.

Did you create
humorous sentences?

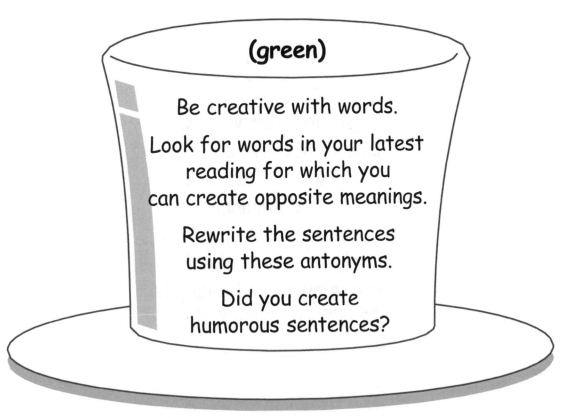

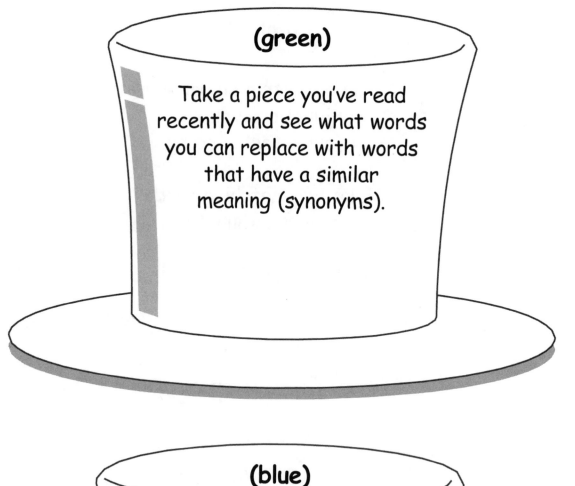

(green)

Take a piece you've read recently and see what words you can replace with words that have a similar meaning (synonyms).

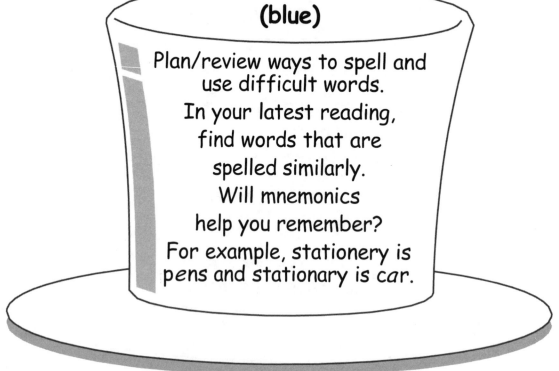

(blue)

Plan/review ways to spell and use difficult words.

In your latest reading, find words that are spelled similarly.

Will mnemonics help you remember?

For example, stationery is pens and stationary is car.

➼ Reading words that have roots in another language can stimulate children to discover more about etymology. For example, many English words begin with the Greek word *aero,* meaning *air.* Children can study many words using the computer program, *Inspiration.*

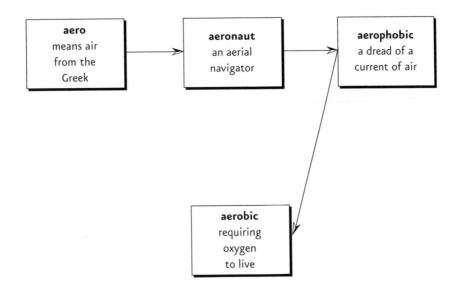

Similar prefixes include *acro, alter, audio, bi, counter, deca, geo,* and *homo.* Some suffixes rooted in another language are *gyro, chrome, cide, derm,* and *gram.*

➼ Make a class or individual *Homophones* book and list in it words that sound the same but have different spellings and meanings. Ask children to look up the word forms and meanings in a dictionary.

Homophones

aloud	allowed	
break	brake	
coarse	course	
hoarse	horse	
knew	new	
oar	or	ore
pair	pear	
to	too	two
would	wood	

➤ Have children research suffixes to find out how they can alter word forms and the meanings by adding suffixes. For example, adding *able* to the verb *enjoy* produces the adjective *enjoyable*. Adding the suffixes *ous*, *ful*, and *less* to a noun also changes the form to an adjective:

marvel (noun)   marvel*ous* (adjective)

event (noun)   event*ful* (adjective)

hope (noun)   hope*less* (adjective)

Other suffixes that change words into adjectives are *al, ed, en, ent, ious,* and *ish*. Adding the suffixes *ment, th, ion,* and *er* to a verb changes the form to a noun:

manage (verb)   manage*ment* (noun)

grow (verb)   grow*th* (noun)

decorate (verb)   decora*tion* (noun)

ski (verb)   ski*er* (noun)

Other suffixes that change verbs into nouns are *ance, ence, ing, ist, nes, ship,* and *tion*.

Children could write sentences using both forms—for example, *marvel* and *marvelous*—and see how the sentences are structured and decide whether meanings have changed or are similar.

Writing and Proofreading

Proofreading is a particular kind of reading in which aspects of writing are carefully examined. A writer who proofreads a composition will check many things—whether it makes sense and conveys the intended message; whether the written piece is structured correctly; and whether the spelling is conventional. Proofreading is an integral part of the writing process, so allow sufficient time for it. The writing focus of language spellers is proofreading and consulting resources in order to correct spelling errors.

Children need to be shown what proofreading spelling involves. By the time children are language spellers, they should have experienced several stages of proofreading. In the early stages, children reread their sentences. After about a year of writing, children are encouraged to circle words they think are incorrectly spelled and later, they circle parts of words they think are incorrect. They may choose one or two words and have another try at correct spelling. At the conclusion of their proofreading, after highlighting errors, they consult a source where they can see the correctly written construction.

Dictionaries serve all sorts of needs; they provide meanings, origins, grammatical forms (parts of speech), variants (synonyms), pronunciations, common phrases, and spelling. The difficulty in using a dictionary to check spelling is that most of the child's spelling of a word needs to be correct. If children's approximations are too far afield, help out by giving a closer approximation. At every opportunity that arises, use a dictionary yourself and demonstrate how you use it. Show children:

- How dictionaries are structured in alphabetical order—the word order in the text and the letter order in each word.
- How parts of speech are shown.
- How to read the meaning.

Being able to use dictionaries is a great support for older children who find recalling patterns of words difficult.

Model Proofreading and Using Dictionaries

➻ Project a transparency of a piece of writing containing misspellings. Give each child a copy of the piece of writing and two different-colored pencils, blue and red. Allow a certain amount of time for the children to make corrections on their sheets in blue pencil. Then, work with the class using the overhead projector and have children mark missed corrections in red. Analyze the children's corrections and overlooked misspellings.

Practice Proofreading

➻ Have children move a piece of firm transparent plastic (trimmed excess lamination is ideal) down the page, line by line, searching only for spelling errors.

➻ Extract portions of texts the children know, rewrite them (double spaced) incorporating appropriate spelling errors, and have the children search for the incorrect spellings. First have them search for particular errors, and as they become more adept, have them search for more general errors. Also encourage them to be aware of correct sentence structure. Here are some examples:

Extract concentrating on one type of spelling error (from *Hannah and the Golden Thread*, by Josephine Croser):

> Carefully, she eased away from the children beside her.
> Molly, the girl who limpd, whimpered and reachd for her.
> The baby, Tim, rolld over and the twins tuggd for an extra
> share of her cloak.

Extract containing many types of spelling errors (from *Hannah and the Golden Thread*, by Josephine Croser):

> Hansy awok with a rush of teror and sat up, tens and alert.
> A nitmar, that's all it was. But not the usuul one where she
> wander alone, searching endlessly.
> This one was about. . . . She didn't realle no. She start to
> tremble and that somehow brok the tension. She lear long ago
> not to cri. Months had pass since that terribl day when Pa had
> been arrest. Far from home, she had had to find way to surviv
> in and around the market, Covent Garden.

Develop Dictionary Skills

➻ Make a class dictionary—a large blank book with twenty-six pages. Write an alphabet letter in large print at the top right-hand corner of each page. To begin, you could cut out large words from magazines and other types of print. Have children, working in groups, glue the words down a column under the appropriate alphabetical heading, leaving spacing between each word. Later they can insert the meanings. As a quick activity each day, have two or three children suggest words they would like to insert in the dictionary. They can choose words from newspapers read at home.

➻ List a number of words beginning with every letter in the alphabet. Make multiple copies of the list. Place children into groups and have them cut out the words and sort them down a column in alphabetical order:

ant

book

cat

➡ Sort words that have the same first letter but different letters for the rest of the words.

damp	dainty
dog	damage
drip	damp

Reinforcement Activities

Prefixes, Common Nouns, Proper Nouns, Collective Nouns, Past Tense Verbs, and Plural Nouns

➡ Using words the class has studied during reading and writing, make:

■ Jigsaw puzzles of prefixes, and see how meanings of words change when prefixes are added.

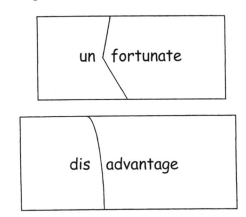

■ Categorizing boards on which children sort different types of nouns, verb tenses ending in *d* and *ed*, and plurals ending in *s* and *es*.

Common Nouns	Proper Nouns	Collective Nouns
book	Cynthia	family
computer	Mount Etna	bunch
girl	Mrs. Singh	herd
shoe	New York	class

ed	d	es	s
look<u>ed</u>	close<u>d</u>	octopus<u>es</u>	picture<u>s</u>
provid<u>ed</u>	state<u>d</u>	witch<u>es</u>	close<u>s</u>
happen<u>ed</u>	place<u>d</u>	express<u>es</u>	provide<u>s</u>
remind<u>ed</u>	abuse<u>d</u>	catch<u>es</u>	judge<u>s</u>

➥ Ask children to record (perhaps in their language journals) what they discovered about certain word forms—what was added, what was not added.

Extend the plural word forms by looking at words that end in *y* and are made plural by changing the *y* to *i* and adding *es*. Let the children answer the question, "Does this always happen?"

Synonyms

➥ Make a set of cards on which are written pairs of synonyms. Have children play a barrier game, in which one child says a word and another finds and states the word with a similar meaning.

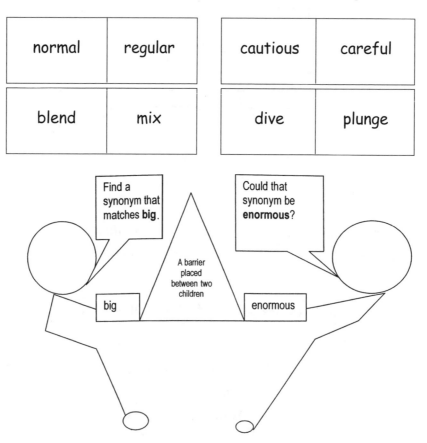

Dictionary Practice

➼ Prepare dictionary problem-solving cards.

Find the longest word.	Find the largest word starting with ____.	Find the first word on page ____.	Search for two words that begin with *al*. Write their meanings.
Find the last word on page ____. Read the meaning and write your own sentence showing you understand the meaning.	Find the first word in the dictionary that begins with *acro* and see where this root *prefix* originated. Write other *acro* words.	Find these words and write the page numbers: *began* *worry* *happen* *apex*	Find three verbs and write sentences that show their meanings.

Word of the Week

➼ Write an unknown word on the white- or blackboard. Have children use dictionaries to find the word, its form, and its meaning. Then ask them to write a sentence to show their understanding.

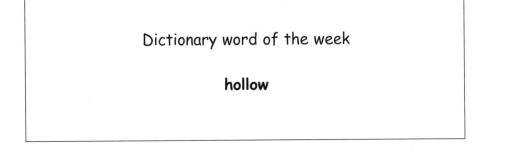

Dictionary word of the week

hollow

Assessment

Analyze children's writing ("thinking hats" assignments, language journal entries, proofreading assignments) using these criteria:

- Are the words spelled correctly?
- Does the child use word forms correctly while constructing sentences?
- Does the child use more complex vocabulary to make the writing interesting?
- Does the child actively proofread, correct spelling, and if necessary add more formal language (adverbs, for example)?

Appendix 1

Spelling Generalizations

Spelling generalizations are another way of discovering and learning the patterns and idiosyncrasies of our language. Carefully choose the rules you bring to the children's attention during reading and writing, because there are frequent exceptions and too many "rules" can complicate spelling.

Generalizations Related to Vowels and Consonants

- When a silent e is placed as an addition at the end of three-letter words, it most often indicates that the short vowel sound is now a long vowel sound: tub, tube.
- Generally the letter *q* is followed by *u*: *queen*.
- The consonants *f*, *l*, and *s* are doubled at the end of most words: *sniff, ball, miss*.
- The consonants *c* and *k* sometimes have the same sound: *cat, kangaroo*.
- The consonants *c* and *k* go together at the end of one-syllable words that have short vowel sounds: *pick*.
- The consonant *s* or *z* at the end of a word is always followed by a silent *e*: *horse, size*.
- Put *i* before *e* after all consonants (*believe*) except after *c*; then it is written *ei*: *receive*. (There are exceptions: *weight, height*.)
- When the words *all, full, fill*, and *till* are added at the beginning or ending of words, one *l* is dropped: *almost, awful, fulfil, until*.
- Usually adjectives ending in *le* form adverbs by dropping the *e* and adding a *y*: *gentle, gently*.

Generalizations Related to Plurals

- To form plurals, add *s* to the end of most nouns: *cows*.
- Add *es* to nouns that end in *ch, sh, o, s, x*, and *z*: *watches, lashes, echoes, classes, foxes, buzzes*. Exceptions are *stomach(s)/monarch(s)* and some words ending in *o*, and *oo*, such as *pianos* and *cockatoos*.
- For a noun ending in *f* or *fe*, change the *f* to *v* and add *es* to form plural: *calf, calves*. There are exceptions: *roof, roofs*.

■ For some nouns, the singular and plural form are the same: *scissors/scissors.*

■ Many nouns form the plural by changing the vowel(s): *man, men, foot, feet.*

Generalizations Related to Suffixes

■ The silent *e* is kept when adding *ly* or *ty*: *lovely, ninety.* There are exceptions: *true, truly.*

■ The *y* is kept when adding the suffix *ing*: *copying.*

■ When adding other suffixes to words ending in *y*—for example, *est, ful, ed*—change the *y* to *i*: *silky, silkiest; pity, pitiful; hurry, hurried.*

■ Adjectives ending in *ant* and *ent* change to *ance* and *ence* in their noun forms: *assistant, assistance; innocent, innocence.*

Generalizations Related to Apostrophes

■ To show omission of letters, add an apostrophe: *they are, they're.*

■ To show possession, add an apostrophe:

   • Singular nouns that do not end in *s*: *dog's bone.*

   • Most singular nouns that do end in *s*: *Chris's book.*

   • Plural nouns that do not end in *s*: *sheep's wool.*

   • Plural nouns that end in *s*: *teachers' workloads.*

Generalizations Related to Capitals

■ Capitals are placed at the beginning of sentences: *Many a night I sat alone.*

■ Capitals are used for proper nouns—for example, names of people, places, or days of the week.

■ Capitals are used at the beginning of adjectives that originate from proper nouns: *American.*

■ Capitalize the pronoun *I.*

Appendix 2
Black Line Masters

Letter Chart

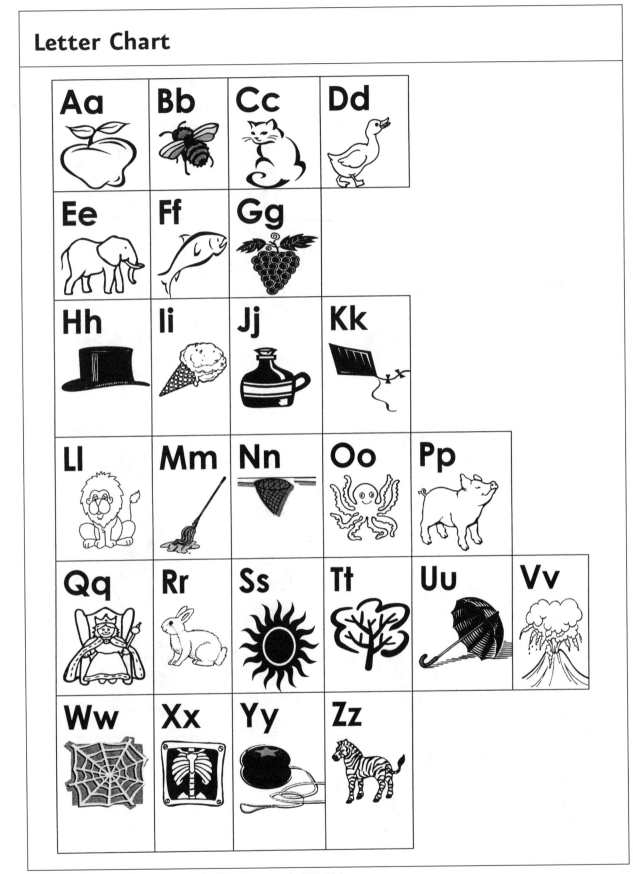

Letter Assessment

Assessment   Write the First Letter

Name: Date:

Letter Knowledge Record

LETTER KNOWLEDGE RECORD

Name _____   Year _____

Beginning Fall Date _____   *Baseline*   *Total*

Recognition a b c d e f g h i j k l m n o p q r s t u v w x y z

Written   a b c d e f g h i j k l m n o p q r s t u v w x y z
Orientation
Difficulties

End Fall Date _____   *Progress*   *Total*

Letters Taught: *l h i b k t r n m*

Recognition a b c d e f g h i j k l m n o p q r s t u v w x y z

Written   a b c d e f g h i j k l m n o p q r s t u v w x y z
Orientation
Difficulties

End Winter Date _____   *Progress*   *Total*

Letters Taught: *p u v w   c o a d*

Recognition a b c d e f g h i j k l m n o p q r s t u v w x y z

Written   a b c d e f g h i j k l m n o p q r s t u v w x y z
Orientation
Difficulties

End Spring Date _____   *Progress*   *Total*

Letters Taught: *g q s e   y f j x z*

Recognition a b c d e f g h i j k l m n o p q r s t u v w x y z

Written   a b c d e f g h i j k l m n o p q r s t u v w x y z
Orientation
Difficulties

Direction   Date _____   Using initial letter in writing   Date _____

One-on-One Matching   Date _____   Knowing concept letter   Date _____

Note: Mark the letter as known when the child quickly recognizes and writes it.

© 2004 by Liz Simon from *Strategic Spelling*. Portsmouth, NH: Heinemann.

High Frequency Words

HIGH FREQUENCY SPELLING RECORD 1

Name:

Focus:

the	I	is	a	to
am	my	we	in	of
and	it	here	on	went
like	he	up	go	are
going	me	can	this	look
for	get	come	so	at
as	got	with	have	you
all	his	day	that	when
they	her	saw	about	him
back	after	said	had	very
down	be	home	not	some
them	was	look	because	into

High Frequency Words

HIGH FREQUENCY SPELLING RECORD 2

Name:

Focus:

there	from	our	what	cat
then	time	will	she	off
could	two	took	over	an
by	their	around	if	who
found	night	see	little	people
do	start	man	us	mom
next	put	ran	did	were
now	door	just	would	told
dad	where	but	old	big
one	no	which	school	out
before	once	place	thought	long
more	car	boat	soon	fell

High Frequency Words

HIGH FREQUENCY SPELLING RECORD 3

Name: ⟶   Focus:

stay	or	asked	good	morning
way	been	police	didn't	away
heard	inside	things	yes	gave
lived	men	boy	walk	plane
friend	until	called	name	other
again	bed	dog	made	first
has	too	lost	white	room
every	play	still	years	tree
how	later	children	know	she
only	Mr.	your	water	through
left	three	don't	happy	another
last	cave	friends	Mrs.	something

High Frequency Words

HIGH FREQUENCY SPELLING RECORD 4

Name: **Focus:**

walked	why	house	girl	while
suddenly	nice	well	find	take
end	out	never	looking	lunch
turn	help	sleep	small	black
much	stopped	decide	five	they
few	money	always	horse	year
days	family	really	also	great
its	dark	head	walking	fire
four	right	slip	finish	hour
knew	o'clock	brother	coming	I'm
make	story	outside	thing	many
tea	ground	best	says	work

Blank Grids

Tic Tac Toe

- Each player chooses words with a different spelling pattern—digraph, blend, prefix, suffix, or visual pattern.

- Each player takes a turn trying to place three words in a row, horizontally, vertically, or diagonally, exemplifying his or her chosen spelling pattern.

TIC TAC TOE

TIC TAC TOE

Spelling Error Analysis

SPELLING ERROR ANALYSIS

Name _____ Date _____

Child's spelling	Text spelling	ANALYSIS	ANALYSIS	
		Sound – initial – medial – ending	Visual – initial – medial – ending	
		Sound – initial – medial – ending	Visual – initial – medial – ending	
		Sound – initial – medial – ending	Visual – initial – medial – ending	
		Sound – initial – medial – ending	Visual – initial – medial – ending	
		Sound – initial – medial – ending	Visual – initial – medial – ending	
		Sound – initial – medial – ending	Visual – initial – medial – ending	
		Sound – initial – medial – ending	Visual – initial – medial – ending	
		Sound – initial – medial – ending	Visual – initial – medial – ending	
		Sound – initial – medial – ending	Visual – initial – medial – ending	
		Sound – initial – medial – ending	Visual – initial – medial – ending	
		Sound – initial – medial – ending	Visual – initial – medial – ending	

Note: A check mark (✔) is assigned to sound *or* visual.

Weekly Plan

FOCUSED SHARED READING OF NARRATIVES—A WEEKLY PLAN

Big book title: Poem/other:

Previous knowledge:

Focus:

Follow-up activity:

Monday: Knowing the story

Tuesday: Introducing the focus

Quickly retell

Read the story

Wednesday: Developing the focus

Quickly retell

Read the story

Thursday: Further developing the focus

Quickly retell

Read the story

Friday:

Fiction: Rereading with minimum interruption and maximum expression and enjoyment

Follow-up activity or assignment

Clusters   Letter groups (patterns) in words—initial blends, digraphs, rhymes, suffixes, prefixes, double letters, etc.

Developmental learning   Beginning with what a child knows and gradually building on that knowledge. A *developmental level* (see next entry) defines where children are currently in their understanding and skills.

Emergent/Early/Transitional   *Developmental levels. Emerging:* awareness of sound and symbol relationships, directional behavior, and one-on-one matching. *Early:* able to write phrases or sentences in which many of the sounds in words are present. *Transitional:* beginning to show awareness of visual parts of words (for example, bec*ause*).

Etymology   The origin of words—for example, from Latin or Greek.

Focus   Specific learning being concentrated on

Grapheme   Visual symbol used in a writing system

Graphophonic   Dealing with the link between the letter and the sound it makes

Lexicon   The words of a language

Logographics   Symbols used to represent words

Morpheme   The smallest meaningful unit of language—for example, prefix *un*, suffix *ly*.

Morphemics   The relationship between meaningful parts of words

Morphology   Study of the form and structure of meaningful parts of words

Orthography   Conventional spelling

Phoneme   A smallest unit of sound in language—for example, the initial phoneme in dog is /d/.

Phonological   Having to do with the system of speech sounds

Phonological and phonemic awareness   The awareness of sounds in words; knowing how to manipulate sounds—for example, changing phonemes (*in, on*), blending phonemes (*f-l-i-p*), and segmenting or hearing the parts of a word (an onset [*c*], a rime [*ar*], syllables)

Phonology   Study of sounds in language

Semantics   Meaning in language

Syntactic   Having to do with sentence construction and grammar

Visual patterns   Recurring letter sequences (*clusters*), in words, including unusual or tricky parts of words:
- silent letters *(gh, k, e)*
- patterns having varied sounds *(ough)*
- *y* making an *e* or *i* sound
- two letters having the same sound—for example, *c* and *k*; double letters
- sound not matching letter sequence—for example, augh, the suffixes ious and sion

Bean, W., and C. Bouffler. 1997. *Spelling: An Integrated Approach*. Victoria, Australia: Eleanor Curtain.

Boehm, A. E. 1986. *Boehm Test of Basic Concepts*. Level B. New York: Psychological Corporation.

Chomsky, N., and M. Halle. 1968. *The Sound Pattern of English*. New York: HarperCollins.

Clay, M. 1993a. *Reading Recovery*. Portsmouth, NH: Heinemann.

Clay, M. 1993b. *An Observation Survey*. Portsmouth, NH: Heinemann.

Croser, J. 1999. *Hannah and the Golden Thread*. Vernon Hills, IL: ETA/Cuisenaire.

De Bono, E. 1992. *Six Thinking Hats*. New York: Little Brown.

Dominie letter books. Carlsbad, CA 92008. Dominie Press Inc.

Fleming, D. 1991. *In the Tall, Tall Grass*. New York: Henry Holt.

Fountas, I., and G. S. Pinnell. 1996. *Guided Reading*. Portsmouth, NH: Heinemann.

Graham, A. 1987. "Angus Thought He Was Big." Vernon Hills, IL: ETA/Cuisenaire.

Hill, S. 1991. *Really Rapt*. South Australia: Era Publications (Big Book version).

Holdaway, D. 1979. *The Foundations of Literacy*. Portsmouth, NH: Heinemann.

Inspiration. 2002. Inspiration Software Inc.

Kid Pix Studio. Broderbund Software, Inc.

Microsoft PowerPoint (Microsoft Office). Microsoft Corporation.

O'Sullivan, O., and A. Thomas. April 2000. *Understanding Spelling*. London: CLPE.

"The Tram Ride." 1984. In *Rigby Tadpoles*. Australia: Rigby Education.

Vaughan, M., and D. Brazell. 2000. *Failed Again.* Crystal Lake, IL: Rigby Education.